Daniel Flickinger Wilberforce

Sherbro and the Sherbros

Or, a Native African's Account of His Country and People

Daniel Flickinger Wilberforce

Sherbro and the Sherbros
Or, a Native African's Account of His Country and People

ISBN/EAN: 9783337124267

Printed in Europe, USA, Canada, Australia, Japan

Cover: Foto ©ninafisch / pixelio.de

More available books at **www.hansebooks.com**

SHERBRO AND THE SHERBROS;

OR,

A Native African's Account of His Country and People.

BY

DANIEL F. WILBERFORCE.

"Whereas thou hast been forsaken and hated, so that no man went through thee, I will make thee an eternal excellency, a joy of many generations." Isa. 60 : 15.

DAYTON, OHIO:
UNITED BRETHREN PUBLISHING HOUSE:
1886.

PREFACE.

The author of this pamphlet is a man whose history must be highly interesting to all friends of the missionary cause. It is fitting that a brief account of his life accompany this work.

DANIEL FLICKINGER WILBERFORCE was born on Sberbro Island, near the mainland, on the west coast of Africa, February 24, 1857, and is therefore now twenty-nine years of age. His parents had been converted to Christianity before he was born, so that he is not, and never has been anything approximating a heathen. His parents, after their conversion, took the name of the great English philanthropist. Rev. D. K. Flickinger (now bishop of the United Brethren in Christ) was then laboring as a missionary in Africa, and the parents named their boy for this man of God.

Late in the year of 1871, Mr. Wilberforce found his way to New York in company with a returning missionary; and shortly after, Mr. Flickinger, by the advice of the Missionary Board, brought young Daniel to Dayton, Ohio, where he was at once placed in the public schools. He passed through the several grades of the District, Intermediate, and High school, and took one year of special studies in Union Biblical Seminary, in seven years. When Mr. Wilberforce graduated from the High School, he received one of the three diplomas of SPECIAL HONOR. His personal bearing, thrilling graduating address, and high standing in his class drew from his many friends and the immense audience present most emphatic outbursts of applause.

After selecting a Christian lady of Dayton for a life companion, Miss Lizzie Harris, to whom he was married October 17, 1878, Mr. Wilberforce sailed for his native land under the auspices of the United Brethren Missionary Society, in the autumn of 1878.

His faith and zeal in the work of preaching the Gospel to his fellow-countrymen soon attracted the attention of all in any way acquainted with the missionary efforts on the Western coast of Africa. To a remarkable degree his health and strength were prolonged. At the close of six years' successful labor, owing to

4

some decline of his own health, and the necessity of a change of climate for a time on the part of Mrs. Wilberforce (her health being greatly impaired), it was deemed wise to return to America for a season of rest, and other needed qualifications for their work in Africa. Accordingly, they sailed for New York in April, 1885. Since their arrival, Mr. Wilberforce has been actively engaged in traveling, preaching, lecturing, and collecting money for the work to which he has consecrated his life.

As Africa is a very sickly country, a knowledge of medicine is almost essential to the successful career of a missionary. Hence, as soon as he returned to Dayton, he began the study of medicine under the tutorship of Dr. William Webster, an eminent practitioner of the city, and in due time he repaired to Cleveland, Ohio, where he pursued with great industry and faithfulness a course of medical lectures, thus fitting himself to go on in the study and practice of the healing art with great usefulness among his native Sherbros. He will sail for Africa again in a few days.

His pamphlet will speak for itself. It has been prepared with great pains by one eminently qualified by experience, culture, and piety for the task. He glories in the Cross as being the true remedy for his countrymen's woes, and is both able and willing to give a reason for the hope that is in him, both for himself and his fellows.

WM. McKEE.

Dayton, Ohio, August 1, 1886.

INDEX.

5

SHERBRO AND THE SHERBROS.

It is more than two hundred and fifty years since the European visited the west coast of Africa for business purposes. His traffic was then in human beings. A wonderful change has taken place; the sons of those who robbed and despoiled Africa, and entailed untold miseries upon her, are now presenting to her the true *panacea* for these woes,—the Gospel. Commercial relations have also changed, so that, instead of cargoes of human souls, we have a growing commerce in palm kernels and oil, ivory, gum, ginger, hides, gold-dust, diamonds, etc. Yet it is surprising that during so many years of intercourse the interior remained closed to the foreigner. While I do not regard lightly the adventures and explorations of Messrs. Baker, Burton, Speke, Grant, and others, who have published and given to the world some knowledge of the people met in their travels through the wilds of Africa, yet it is but fair to say it is only recently that, through the labors of the great Dr. Livingstone, and explorations and accounts given by Mr. Stanley, that the foreigner has been permitted to gaze into the interior of a country, marvelous in its extent and vast resources; the grandeur of its natural scenery, with a soil capable of the highest development.

Has not the God whose hand hath led the nations, permitted that country to remain so long unknown that Christianity might achieve her greatest triumphs in the dark continent? The fact alone that the valley of the Congo was opened, and the "Free State" established, the leading nations of the world consenting, without the shedding of one drop of blood in war, seems to me the beginning of triumphs.

The population is variously estimated. Until more accurate statistics are obtained, we must be satisfied to place our population at 250,000,000. Two hundred and fifty millions of beings, created in God's image to hear the gospel, is a fact that ought to awaken the church of Christ to a just sense of its responsibility and the immensity of the field to be occupied.

The country on the west coast is, for the most part, low and almost level, (there are exceptions), but the land rises gradually toward the interior, and there we have the same variety in soil that you find elsewhere. This fact has led some to believe that the interior higher locations are much more to be preferred for health, even for the European or American.

The people are divided into various tribes, speaking different dialects, and differing somewhat in respect to customs, manners, and dispositions. A marked difference in physical appearance and intellectual capacity is apparent to an observant mind. Upward of 400 dialects are spoken. The Veys, or Gallinas tribe, has reduced its dialect to a written language.

Some of the tribes found on or near the coast are known as Foolahs, Mandingo, Soosoo, Limbah, Timneh, Sherbro, Mendi, Lok-Koh, Vey, Bassa Kro, Aku, Ebo, etc. In treating this subject I shall speak almost wholly of the Sherbro people and the neighboring tribes, Mendi and Timneh.

¿ II.   LOVE OF COUNTRY AND COUNTRYMEN.

It was my fortune to be born in Africa, of African parentage. I am identified with the Sherbro people, although my father belongs to another tribe. I share with my people the humiliating thought of our benighted condition. And, painful as it is to speak of my heathen brethren and their condition, yet, if I can by this arouse you to give expression to your sympathy, or in any way tend to hasten the glad day of gospel light, I shall cheerfully undergo its mortification.

I am aware that any attempt to present a picture of heathen life must fall far short of the reality. Especially is it a condition difficult for you to imagine, surrounded as you are by comforts and the blessings of life, and with the influences of a Bible Christianity.

¿ III.   WORK OF UNITED, BRETHREN.

The church of the United Brethren in Christ has its mission in the territory of the Sherbro people of the west coast. Sherbro proper is an extensive country. It lies immediately below Sierra Leone, and north of Liberia, about 6° to 8° north of the equator, and includes what are known as the Ribbee, Bompeh, Plantain and Cockborough, Bargroo, Impereh, Jong,

Boom, and Kittim territories. The dialects of the country are Sherbro, but the dialects of neighboring tribes, Mendi and Timneh, and few others, are extensively spoken. The country is thickly populated. The inhabitants live in towns and villages, the larger and greater number of towns being found away from the coast. Each town has its headman or chief, while each district and territory has its chieftain. This crowding of the people into towns is for protection. Here they sleep and have their homes. During the farming season those who do farm-work go out and work during the day, but return to the town at night. Those whose farm-work carries them a great distance often build temporary sheds, and there stay a part of the time, or during the entire farm season. The houses, as a rule, are closely built together. This is especially so in large towns that must be fortified during a time of war.

The construction of a native house is very simple. The tools required are an ax and matchet, or cutlass. These are to be used for cutting posts, rafters, ropes, bamboo or palm branches, or grass for covering the house. A hoe must be added, with which to dig the clay. The posts are set in holes in the ground, and so cut or forked at the top as to support the beams laid across. These are secured with ropes, the rafters are thrown up so as to meet around a central post at the top, thus making an acute angle, if the house is a round one, or they rest upon a cross-bar if it is rectangular in form. The rafters are lathed and covered with palm branches or grass, or with a kind of shingles made of bamboo leaves pinned together. Between the posts are inserted small sticks; this is a peculiar process of lathing. The body of the building is then ready for the clay, which is applied externally as well as internally. A house like this, if cared for, the roof kept in order, may stand ten or fifteen years, indeed would last longer, if it was not for the white ants that eat the wooden portion of the building. Some of the inhabitants of Sherbro island enclose the sides of their huts with mats made of bamboo reeds.

A wall several feet high, or palisades three to four in number, serves as a fortification. Sentinels keep close watch through the night. This precaution is necessary, for the war-boys in this part of the coast seldom attack during the day, nor do they meet as regularly-organized armies in open field to battle.

You will understand from this statement that wars are of frequent occurrence between the tribes. The stronger and more restless ones will attack
the weaker, and these wars are not so much to avenge wrongs as for the
purpose of plunder. The prisoners of war may be men, women, and children, who are afterward retained as slaves, or sold, and, in the case of
the women, sometimes forced to become the wives of their captors.
In a visit made into the Mendi country, I saw the remains of a peculiar
prison that had been occasionally used for captives taken in war. It had
been the property of a noted warrior, who, because of his many successes
in his campaigns, was said to have help from his "devil." The prison was
an immense hollow tree, with an aperture a number of feet from the ground,
reached by a ladder. Prisoners destined to a sacrifice to this devil were
cast into this tree and left to starve to death. "The dark places of the
earth are filled with the habitations of cruelty."

§ IV. LAWS AND GOVERNMENT.

An important point of interest in each town is the chief's barra, a building different from the rest and generally larger, having a roof, but open on
all sides. In this barra the chief and his advisers, or elders, of the town
are found. This is the first point visited by the stranger when he comes to
a town; for he must make his presence known to the chief, and "shake
his hands," before he can find a resting-place. Here public councils are
held, cases of dispute argued; for, while there are no written laws regu-
lating the conduct of citizens, the rights of men are regarded, and the people
controlled by customs and laws that have been handed down by the fathers.
Very seldom do we hear of murders among native Sherbros, and such
scenes as you read about in your daily journals, that are so common here,
are unusual. The slightest as well as the gravest offenses are carried before the chief, and there argued ; if necessary, lawyers plead, and some of
them are eloquent. The matter is then decided by the chief, if alone,
or by himself and council. This decision is, as a rule, final. Occasional
laws are proclaimed by the *Purrow*, the chief secret-society of the country.
Such laws are general. Cases of theft are decided in various ways.
Murders, when they occur at all, are settled by taking the life of the
murderer, or he may be given up to the friends of the murdered person,
who may do with him as they think best,— kill him or sell him and his

family as slaves. The question has been asked me many times, "Is it your opinion that the heathen will meet a future punishment?" Possibly not, because of the mere fact of their being *heathens*. Yet we must first decide whether heathen nations do not have some standard by which they know this or that to be right or wrong; and if so, whether they live up to their own standard, for by that we must judge them. The Bible answer to the question is given in Romans, 2 : 14. "When the Gentiles which have not the law do by nature the things contained in the law, these having not the law are a law unto themselves; which shew the law written in their hearts (or, the work of the law in their hearts), their consciences also bearing witness, and their thoughts, the meanwhile, accusing or else excusing one another."

§ V. HUSBANDS AND WIVES.

I would not have you infer that we catch all our wives in war. Each man may engage his wife according to the country fashion. This is done as follows: Friends of the man wishing a wife visit the home of the parents or relatives of the girl to be engaged; the "wine-money" or present is paid for the girl. Here customs vary with tribes, and even with families. Some are particular as to the person making the application, a few ask the girl's consent, but, as a rule, the decision of parents is final. We pay much attention to, and regard as binding upon us what our parents say. Occasionally girls are engaged quite young, but do not go to their husbands for years after.

Polygamy is a custom of the country, and it is a common occurrence for men to have any number of wives, from one up. I have known men who had over one hundred wives. But you must take into consideration the fact that the African does not look upon this thing as a crime or sin; to him it is the custom received from his ancestors, and his social standing or influence is enhanced in proportion to the number of slaves and wives he has. The women, on the other hand, often regard it a matter whereof to be proud to be called the "king's wives," or the wives of a "big man." Neither regard it as a crime against society, nor do they see that true love can not exist under the system of polygamy, nor can fathers have that natural affection for their children; that by it womanhood is debased, jealousies incited, not only among the women, but children of the same father and different mothers, and that unfaithfulness must be a necessary outgrowth. I can say, however, that most of the young ladies who have come under Christian influence have refused to accept polygamous engagements; some have, however, been forced by their own parents to submit.

The lot of woman is everywhere a hard one, till that condition is ameliorated by the influences of a pure Christianity. In Africa her condition is no exception; indeed, if anything, it is worse. She is married not because she is considered the equal and fit companion for her husband, but to serve his pleasure; and if in return for this service she should receive the most unkind treatment, she has no redress.

I once saw a women who had a rope around her neck, her hands tied behind her back, the other end of the rope in the hands of a man who was beating her. I supposed first that she was a slave. When I remonstrated with him for this brutal conduct upon the highway, he said it was all right; she was his wife, had run away, and now that he had got her back he would "learn her sense." I have heard and read of men in your civilized country who undertook to teach their wives sense by beating them; the law took the matter in hand, and in turn taught them sense. But in the case referred to, the chief of the town had given permission.

Ladies of America, let me make an appeal to your sympathy for the women of my country, many of whom from the nature of things are my own relatives; for you can help them if you will. "What can you do?" Send to them, to their country, the Gospel; it is the balm for every woe. Educate them; elevate the young people, the girls, who are to become the mothers of the future; give them such a training as will make them intelligent, virtuous and industrious wives and mothers; educate for them the boys who are to become their husbands—make them Christian men, fit companions for their wives.

Our ladies in Africa are intelligent and industrious. In cases where they are rulers of towns and country, they have shown skill and tact equal to most men and superior to many.

¿ VI. HOMES.

The homes of our people are the rudely constructed huts previously described, with little or no furniture. But our more civilized natives display good taste in building and making their homes comfortable and attractive. Indeed, some have built splendid residences.

The principal article of food is rice. Cassava, sweet-potatoes, yams, cocoa, etc., are cultivated to some extent; also tropical fruits, as oranges, bananas, pine-apples, mangoes, guavas, and many more. Our "bill of fare" is not extensive, nor does it call for many cooking utensils or dishes. We use no stoves as a rule, but our cooking is done in open fire-places, while the pot or sauce-pan rests upon three stones or supports. For fuel we use wood.

To prepare a first-class meal you want rice, fish or chicken, palm-oil, salt, onions or yarbas, and pepper; the latter is indispensable. The rice as it comes from the farm must first be carefully hulled. This is done in a wooden mortar, and the rice pounded with a stick or wooden pestle. This is done by women and children. It is then boiled in sauce-pans or pots as only African women can prepare rice. The stew may consist of chickens, fish, or anything that may come within the range of one's taste. Sometimes the meat is made into palaver sauce,—a dish that must be tasted to know what it is. If my commendation is worth anything, I can vouch for its palatableness. This or the stew is prepared in a separate vessel. The rice is then served, generally rice and stew served in one dish, sometimes separately. I must say our African ladies excel in the preparation of a rice meal. One or more persons eat out of a dish or bowl. Instead of the slow process of eating with a knife and fork, we prefer to use that instrument that was given us for the purpose,— the hand. The foofoo is a preparation from the cassava, and is eaten with palaver sauce, but is one of those things that are really pleasant to taste, but hard to describe. The best thing about a native meal is that it costs so little. In an ordinary-sized family, such a meal as I have described may cost from two to five cents per individual. It is possible to live in Freetown for five to ten cents a day. You must understand that we can be extravagant, sometimes, with food, as you are in this country. The more wealthy ones and people of Freetown, who have acquired different tastes, often have a bill of fare something like yours. At any rate, they know how to prepare them, as our wedding-feasts at Shaingay and other places have proven.

§ VII. HOSPITALITY.

No people show greater hospitality to strangers than do Africans. The first act of hospitality is to give the stranger water in which to bathe. Native-made cloth must be provided, even though he may have brought his own. Food is supplied him as long as he continues a guest. But to secure this attention and good will, it is necessary to comply with the custom of "shaking the chief's hand," which is required of strangers, both Africans and foreigners.

During my stay in Africa I made several trips, visiting very many towns within reach from all our principal stations, twice going beyond the Sherbro territories. The first trip was made in 1881, to the Yawnie territory; the second to the Mendi country, during January, 1885; the expense attending both being borne by myself. As the Mendis and Yawnies are regarded as the most restless and warlike of the tribes of our part of Africa, I shall here give examples of their conduct toward strangers. I had formed the ac-quaintance of a chieftain of the Mendi country, who gave me a hearty invitation to visit him, saying, also, that his chief, the late Carjoe, of that territory, would be pleased to see me, as they had already heard about me. On reaching the country, I repaired to the residence of my friend, the sub-chief, who at once informed Carjoe of my arrival. To honor the stranger, the chief called to see me. We "shook hands" formally, I giv-ing several yards of goods, which he accepted thankfully, but declined hearing anything I had to say as to my business till he should give tokens of welcome. Said he: "I can't talk business with a hungry stranger, hence I must first look for something for you to eat." So I was left in the care of his sub-chief, who, for our entertainment in a small way till the return of the chief, provided a goat and basket of rice already hulled. Two days afterward the chief came in state, attended by a retinue of women and men, the former his wives (for he had about two hundred). One woman carried his gun on her shoulder, another carried his sword, a third his shot-pouch, a fourth his parasol, while a male-servant, whose place was to sit at the chief's feet, carried a bunch of keys. Several others carried baskets of rice, two pieces of cloth of native manufacture, and a large sheep. "This small (?) quantity of rice," he said, "will enable you to get strength after your long journey. And the sheep you may roast, instead of a chicken, till I can get you something better." When I left him some days later,— rather too soon to get the "cow" that was to have been killed for my entertainment,— he gave six country-made cloths to be used for my comfort during the return home. I wish to say here that Carjoe wielded a strong power in that country. There are nine large towns, built closely together, each having its fortifications, and except the one in which the chief him-self lives, governed by a sub-chief. These towns have thousands of human beings living without a certain knowledge of God. They are capabie of a most rapid development, and should have the gospel.

From the incidents already cited, you may see how large-hearted our heathen brethren are. Even our wildest war boys are not lost to feelings for the comfort of the stranger.

While I was at Rotufunk in the year 1881, we learned that the Yawnies were threatening the Bompeh people, particularly those at Rotufunk, for allowing missionaries to settle there. Whether the reasons given were the real cause for the emnity, I am unable to say. But one thing was certain, the Mohammedans, who had made Rotufunk a slave depot, fearing that the slave trade would in time be seriously affected, did not lose their opportunity to stir up enemies. I decided to go up to that country and in some way have the people become acquainted with us, and the real object of missionary enterprises. I took an interpreter (for I could not speak the Timinee,) and a few school-boys. A band of warriors from that region who had come down to trade, learning of my proposed visit to their country, offered to act as escorts. A previous acquaintance with the "Yawnie boys" did not inspire me with the tenderest feelings toward them. It was as follows: we were conducting a Sabbath-evening service in a barra, and had commenced singing, when I heard a band of singers (attracted, I suppose, by our singing,) coming toward our meeting-place. I rather congratulated myself that our stranger friends, to whom we had extended a most cordial invitation that evening, would be among my listeners; and though they were coming with much noise, I thought we could stop it when they entered the barra. Imagine our feeling and the confusion when, instead of taking seats, one of them, a leader, unsheathed his sword and brandished it as if determined upon "business." They did not tarry long, but kept on singing their war song till they passed out of the barra through another opening. They were Yawnies I afterward learned, made drunk with the "white man's rum."

You can appreciate my feelings when these warriors from the same country insisted that they *must* accompany me as escorts to their chief. I reluctantly consented. We had gone but a short distance when some one proposed that the "white man" (meaning civilized or a man who speaks English) be borne in a hammock. Of course, I declined and walked. We decided to spend the night in a small village near the boun-dary line of the Bompeh and Yawnie territories. On reaching the town a hut was assigned me, and almost immediately after I heard our warriors singing a war song and marching about the village. Soon two of them brought a chicken. "This," they said, "is for our stranger; he is the guest of our Chief Pah Senna, and we mean to take good care of him, for the chief will call us in question for any lack of attention. We are not in our territory yet, but if you should see anything, even a cow, and should want it you have only to tell us and we will get it for you." The boys who were with me had another chicken given them. Dinner was prepared, and after thanks to Him from whom all blessings flow (I felt it was from Him, tho' the devil brought it,) I began to devour my chicken with all the zeal of a hungry man. I had been at this task some little time when I heard a noise in the town, and a few moments after one of our boys came running, "Please sir, we done got in trouble. They are making a 'rowl' about the chickens." I never could tell afterward why I did not leave my food and go settle the "rowl." But I didn't till I finished my meal, and before I went out the matter had been settled by the warriors who told the people about their distinguished stranger, and that it was the duty of the people of the town to entertain him, but as they did not meet them in the town they had undertaken that duty for them. This explanation seemed reasonable, and so the matter ended. I assure you, after this chicken "rowl" I never mentioned "cow" to them, although I saw several, for I was certain they would get it, even if somebody had to suffer for it. The utmost attention was given us, and entertainment provided for by their savage chief. At the end of seven days I left them, no one asking pay for house or food that had been provided during my journey and stay among them.

§ VIII. AFRICAN CHILDREN.

Boys and girls, I must tell you something about the Sherbro children, to whom you have sent missionaries. When a boy or girl is born, papa and mamma don't have to go through a long catalogue of grand-fathers and grand-mothers or uncles and aunts for generations to find a suitable name, for our little fellows come into the world with their names. The first son of

every female is called *Cho;* the second *Thong*, and names for any number
of boys. The first girl *Boye;* the second, *Yeymah*, etc. From this very
handy arrangement some of you boys are either *Chos*, *Thongs*, *Saus*, or
Barkys, and some girls *Boyes* or *Yeymahs*. Sometimes we have a good
many *Chos* in the same family, or *Boyes*, because they may be children cf
one father but different mothers. In that case something must be added
when they have to distinguish between them; more frequently the mother's
name is added. The writer's name, according to this arrangement, is *Sau;*
you can easily pronounce it, for it is like "Saul" with the "l" dropped
off. Now there are a good many cousins who may have the name *Sau;*
to distinguish mine when I used to visit my relatives, I would be called
Sau-Coyah, *Coyah* being my mother's country name.

In most cases before our children are fully grown, they enter or are
forced to become members of some one of the native secret organizations,
where they lose their former names and receive new ones. *Cho* or *Thong*
may become *Bangang*, *Beah*, or something else; and *Boye* or *Yeymah*
may be *Sateah* or *Yaing Kain*.

Instead of being rocked in cradles, the little child is carried about upon
its mother's back, to which it is bound with a cloth. From the quiet it
restores to a restless child, you may believe the little one finds no bed as
easy as its living cradle.

Though there are no schools, except such as are opened by missionaries,
our children have many ways of spending their time. You are not the
only children in the world who play "hide and seek," or who jump ropes,
climb trees, make traps for birds, catch fish, go fruit hunting and swim-
ming, for children the world over are the same as to the various ways by
which they enjoy themselves.

They are as happy a set of children as you can find anywhere, for
although they have not fine things and beautiful homes, and though most
of them sleep on mats spread upon the floor, they are perhaps more con-
tented than some of you are, except when the *drivers* or traveling ants get
into their homes and they have to get up and leave the house to them, then
they are not happy; for nobody likes to be forced out of bed at midnight
and be even driven out of home, because somebody with more fight in
him, or more numerous, wants possession.

2

As they grow stronger, they must help to hull the rice, carry water for home use,* get wood, and during the "bird driving" season help to keep the birds from eating or destroying the rice. They never grow too old to obey their parents; indeed, not only their own parents, but older persons in general. Some of you stop at twenty-one; we are *never free* from the obligations that rest upon us. Father and mother have the same claim and right to command at our age of fifty as they had when we were little children.

Evenings are spent in various ways—in songs and dance, with or without drums or rattling gourds; or somebody, famed for telling stories or fables about big devil, wonderful people, intelligent animals, etc., entertains them by these fables, interspersed with solos and choruses, in which young and old participate. I can remember how I used to take in these horrible stories, which were of such extreme interest, that we would afterward be so affected by them that for days we trembled in the darkness, and avoided the loneliest places.

In places where war is considered a profession, our boys learn early to wield the sword, or whatever the principal arms may be. Our Sherbro children have not much of that to do.

In a few places day and Sabbath schools have been opened, and the children have made rapid progress, both in school-work and in the acquisition of the English. Not all the children of the towns attend school. Some are slaves, and others can't come because they have nothing to wear. In some of our stations we are often obliged to go to the nearest village to get the children for the Sabbath-school. In this work our school-boys have rendered good service, in bringing to us quite a number of children. The naked ones have gowns put on them, which are taken off when school is over. You see, we are obliged, in many cases, to clothe children when they come to our schools, for heathen children do not wear clothes until they are grown to a good size.

Many of our children, some very young, have become Christians, and most of them are members of the seekers' classes. That some of them have taken a Christian stand in advance of their parents may be seen from the following: Madeline, a girl of our mission and some time ago a member

* In our heathen towns wells are not common, but the water for drinking and cooking purposes is obtained from springs or streams near which the town is located. The water is carried in kettles or vessels of wood or clay.

of the seekers' class, was, a few months ago, with others, baptized. A few days after, the father came to the mission in quite a rage, and accosting Brother Gomer, asked: "You done make my picken drink God-water?" "I baptized Madeline," was the reply. Again he asked angrily, "How can you do a thing like that when I born the gal, and she has already drank country medicine?" To this and much more Mr. Gomer, who has quite a tact in dealing with natives, listened quietly, and finally asked the enraged father: "Are you done?" "Yes." "Then who has the girl in charge?" "You got um," replied he. "Very well, then," said Brother G.; "if my medicine passes your own, it must do good, but you must go sit down first until we see." The father went away, still repeating: "This thing you do me is not good."

The faithfulness of the children, as well as the advantage of taking and educating the boys and girls in the mission family, is evident from the following: *Bentoo*, or Dorcas, a girl who had been with Mrs. Gomer some years, was recently sent for by her mother, an invalid. who earnestly wished to see her daughter quickly, because she (the mother) was very sick. Mrs. Gomer consented; but it was afterward found that the mother wished to give her as wife to a man who had paid something for the girl (without Dorcas's knowledge). Dorcas refused, saying she was a mission girl. The wife of the man pleaded with the girl to consent to live with her husband. The man got ugly and threatened, but Dorcas was firm, and said, "When I am ready for one, I will marry my own husband," whereupon she picked up her bundle and walked all the way to the mission.

Mr. Gomer, writing to me about this incident, added: "You must lay special stress upon the importance of training up the mothers of the country in mission families. Some say because girls can't work on a farm don't take them in the mission, but that is not my decision."

§ IX. ANIMALS, INSECTS, OYSTERS.

I might tell you about our African animals and insects, for there are many peculiarities found among them. You would think it funny to see a sheep without wool, and just so our children would think your sheep strange-looking creatures. Then you never saw oysters grow on trees, but such sights are common to our children, for they often gather lots of them; yes, real oysters. But I haven't time to explain all these things, and yet I must talk about *ants*. You know these little insects are found in almost every country, because Solomon, the wisest man of Bible history, calls the attention of lazy folks to their industry. In Africa, where we have different species of them, I have seen striking examples of their industry and perseverance. Such hardships and discouragements as would seem to overcome us don't at all daunt their courage or try their patience. We used to break down their buildings, and it would be surprising how earnestly and steadily they would work to repair the damage done them. In warm countries they are very numerous, and of different species, some so small that you can barely see them with the naked eye, and others may be larger, even three fourths of an inch in length. These ants are all peculiar. The *Drivers*, that travel in bands, and visit houses, and attack men and animals, would surprise you by their movements. There is the line of march, where perfec: order is observed; then, when the presence of an enemy is suspected, the reconnoitering force is ordered out, and if you happen to be the suspected party, you are soon made to feel that you must either fall back or fight. If you insist upon it, orders are sent to headquarters, and the force marshalled to battle. A leopard even can't stand before them. Our largest animals fear them. Then, too, when they reach a house or place where they have heard they may find food, immediately every soldier becomes a foraging party. Roaches, centipedes, scorpions, rats, and all insects begin to run for life. The best thing you can do, then, is to leave the house to them, for as soon as they get what they want, or have gone through to see what is in your building, the line of march is again formed, and off they go.

The most wonderful species of the ant is the *white ant or Termites*. We in Africa call them *bug-a-bugs*. As the name Termites implies, they are very destructive, and will destroy in a short time houses, fences, and everything made of wood, even books and clothing, if they can get to them. They must be watched closely. There are two kinds of *bug-a-bugs*,—a small and a large one. You often see the houses of the small kind rising from one to three feet in height, made of clay, something like a column with a conical shaped roof. I think they add to this height every year, so that the height depends upon their age. These are the sacred ants that are worshiped by our people, because they believe spirits exist in their houses.

The larger kind are more numerous. Their houses are built on a different plan, being wide at the base and pointed at the top, sometimes looking very much like the pictures you see of the pyramids. They are good architects, as the outside is adorned with domes and steeples of different sizes and shapes. These hills or buildings run up as high as twelve to fifteen feet. The interior of these hills is wonderful in the ingenious arrangement of halls and chambers, and passages of different sizes and every imaginable shape. In these hills you meet different classes of citizens. First, is the queen, who, when full-grown is about four inches in length and one inch in diameter. In the center of the hill is a winding passage leading to her apartments. I have been told that she is borne through this passage into different parts of the palace during different hours of the day. The queen herself lives in a small mud palace, with scarcely room for her to turn in. I have never seen any door, but I have noticed small holes which are for the workers who wait on her majesty, as they have to go in and out to feed her, and possibly to carry her orders to different parts of this huge dwelling. If a queen dies or is removed the colony breaks up. Second, are the soldiers, one-half or three-fourths of an inch long,—queer looking soldiers with large heads, nearly half their whole length. They are brave and fierce, and can bring blood every time they bite. I have fought them and have the utmost respect for them. Third, are the workers, who build and repair this dwelling and do the work necessary. They are about one-fourth to one-half inch long. One curious thing about these ants and one, the philosophy of which I can not explain now, is that in certain seasons they come out with wings, great numbers of them, and fly about for some time, then drop their wings at the trunk of a tree or stump.

Did I say oysters grew on trees? Well, I must explain. We have along the sea shore vast tracts of muddy swamps, covered with groves of Mangrove trees. These trees are peculiar in that some of their roots come from the branches at the top and grow downward till they reach the ground. Then a new tree makes a start. Sometimes these roots dip into the water instead of in the mud, and on these limbs little oysters fasten themselves and grow ; all we need to do is to cut off a limb and we have a thick bunch of oysters. Is not ours a peculiar country? There are yet other wonderful things, but I have not time to mention them.

§ X. FARMS.

The soil for the most part is productive, capable of yielding in abundance rice, cassava, potatoes, cocoa, yams, corn, coffee, cotton, etc., yet farming is done to a limited extent. You nowhere see beautifully laid off farms, such as greet the eye everywhere throughout your extensive country. The greatest portion of the land is covered with a dense growth, with extensive forests here and there. A new place is chosen and cleaned off each year, while the farm of the present season must be left to grow again into brush during three or four years before it is cleared again for planting.

The implements used are a matchet or cutlass, ax and hoe; these being small and rudely made, can not do thorough work. It is no wonder that the amount of food products realized is proportionately inadequate to meet the average wants of the inhabitants.

To become an independent people, Africans must first learn to produce more than they consume. Hence if you will benefit Africa, and bring about those conditions necessary to make a people prosperous, train our young people in the industrial branches. The African is not insensible to personal comforts, and when properly instructed in agricultural and industrial pursuits, he will desire to live as a converted and industrious being; will have better farms, build better homes (for in civilized localities splendid buildings have already been erected), and the battle will then have been half fought; for Christianity can thrive better and take deeper root in a soil so prepared. For the accomplishment of this purpose, better implements must be introduced.

It has been said of Africans that "they are too lazy to work." You must qualify this statement if you take into consideration the fact that a *heathen condition* is one that spreads about it an influence which affects the whole being, morally, spiritually, physically. You can never fully estimate the energetic life of a people till you give them a favorable atmosphere. Christianize Africa, educate her sons and daughters; in other words, set in motion the hidden life; then (with due allowance for climatic effects) *bring your verdict.*

One traveling through the country sees a good deal of idleness, it is true. At the same time he sees most of the inhabitants at some employment. Some spin cotton, weave cloth with looms that are their own construction, make mats, baskets, and various articles, sometimes displaying remarkable taste and ingenuity; or they are on farms, or gathering palm nuts, extracting the oil, or breaking palm kernels for market. We must not forget that the ship loads of kernels, oil, and other products sent to Europe every month, are first prepared by natives and brought to the merchant for sale; sometimes brought in hampers, borne upon the back of natives, who come from towns many miles in the interior.

You hear sometimes that "African women do all the work on farms." The inference must be that the men do nothing. Farm-work may, for convenience, be divided into three stages. First, the " bush-cutting " stage, when the land selected must be cleared of its dense growth and large trees. It is the men who do this work. With thorns and vines, sharp blades to wade through, often cutting into the skin, this may be considered the most trying and dangerous stage of farm-work. The work of the women during this stage is to provide and prepare food for the men in the " bush." After the land has been burned over, and while the men are getting ready the hoes for planting rice, the women plant the cassava. Children often help in this work. The second, or "rice-planting" stage, is shared by men and women, but the men are always in the majority; the women found among them are generally slaves. The women, after this, become wholly responsi ble for keeping the weeds from growing among the rice, till harvest. This is tedious work, involving much exposure to severe weather. The men, at this time, are employed in repairing war-fences, building or repairing huts or gathering the palm-nuts from the trees. Some do a good deal of fishing or hunting, or the time is idled away. The third, or " rice-cutting " stage, is shared by all,— men, women, and children. Neighbors sometimes lend help to each other. With the exception of the tediousness of cutting each stem separately, "rice-cutting" is the most pleasant work on the farm. It means " little work and plenty to eat."

§ XI. RELIGIONS AND INSTITUTIONS.

The religions are pagan and Mohammedan. The pagan has an idea of God; he recognizes a supreme power. I have never found any tribe of people who have not so much as an idea of God. The Sherbro man speaks of Him as *Hobahtokch*, the Mendi man calls him *Ngewoh*, or *Ngewoh wah*, terms expressive of the Great One above. Being the essence of goodness itself, and not disposed to harm his creatures, the pagan does not realize any necessity to worship Him. The devil is supposed to possess supreme power, also, and is concerned with the affairs of men, and his demands are many, (to keep him at peace it must be done) sometimes requiring human sacrifices. These must be given, even though by the giving of them the heart be made to bleed. The demon is capable of assuming various forms, either of men or animals; and, whether derived from tradition as connected with man's primeval history, I am unable to say, but it is strange that the form that he is often supposed to assume is that of a serpent.

The spirits of the dead are also appeased and their co-operation secured by preparing food for them or offering sacrifices of fowls and animals. This does not suffice; charms and greegrees are procured to ward off evil or sickness, or thwart the designs of enemies and witches. Recognize in this effort, ye friends of humanity, the struggle to which man is doomed, that even a heathen feels the presence and power of evil. In his struggles an inventive mind is ever pointing out *some* way of escape; hence,

"The heathen, in his blindness,
Bows down to wood and stone."

From this labyrinthian darkness, who can escape unless directed by a power more than human? It is fearful to talk about the salvation of the heathen without the Gospel. You in the land of Gospel light, may be lulled to sleep under the sense of carnal security, not so with us, who are in darkness. Our condition is not one of peace and safety, but of despair. We are lost in a maze of superstitious notions. We have tried the rivers, we have trusted greegrees, we have appealed to charms, and have worshipped idols and devils. All have failed us; we have no peace, no hope.

The pagan occasionally speaks of retribution after death. Several years ago, a warrior of an interior district, who had become noted for both his exploits and deeds of extreme cruelty, died. Many fancied they saw smoke or mist arise from the grave, and attributed this to the fact that the wicked warrior was being punished for his cruelties. Again, it is not unusual to hear pagans talk of a "clean road" after death. But, alas! these are thoughts which only disquiet a soul, but afford no light to those who "sit in the valley and shadow of death."

The Mohammedan recognizes only "One God," and Mohammet as the true prophet. He despises the pagan because of his idols, and yet is himself a manufacturer of charms or greegrees for which he claims supernatural power. This religion wields a mighty influence in many parts of Africa. In almost every town may be found one or more Mohammedan priests, who are sometimes looked upon as doctors and respected for the power that they claim is vested in them. If a war campaign is to be set in motion the priest must be employed to "cook the war;" that, is to insure the safety and success of the warriors, cause confusion in the ranks and councils of the enemy by sending a curse upon them. Warriors have been known to scale barricades, face the guns of the enemy (which are not always in a condition to do much harm), because they wore about them a charm especially prepared for the occasion. If their lives were lost in battle, they either must have done contrary to the orders given with the charms, or their time for death had come.

This sect presents numerical strength, having representatives in almost every tribe of Africa, some tribes being almost wholly Mohammedan in faith or in sentiment. Where strong in numbers they erect mosques and conduct schools, hence most of their priests are learned in the Arabic language, which they read and write with ease. Among them are found men who are conscientious in all they do, and who sometimes denounce the practices of their unscrupulous brethren. The greater number are polygamists, slave - masters and traders, and dealers in charms that they for the most part know do not contain the efficacious influence attributed to them. Feeling their superiority in point of letters they despise manual labor as only fit for women and slaves, hence they do no work, but very many travel from place to place and obtain their livelihood by trading (often in human beings), doctoring, or by making charms or gregrees. Sometimes noted Mohammedans are sent for from distant places to help chieftains who believe they can assist them. We must not underestimate the work that the Church must do to overcome this influence, yet with the dawn of light and truth and under the penetrating rays of the sun of righteousness, Mohammedanism is beginning to realize that its sway so long held is disputed by no mean power. Hence the complaints and charges often alleged against the Christian missionary. The words of a Mohammedan friend, "You done spoil the people," or words of similar import, are an admission which only a sense of danger to their principles has forced from them. The distribution or sale of Bibles and Testaments ought to be encouraged, as a work of that kind may lead to grand results, for most of our Mohammedans read a Bible with interest even if only because it is printed in Arabic, a language to them sacred.

§ XII. MOHAMMEDAN DECEPTION.

During a short stay at an inland mission I was one evening invited to witness a peace sacrifice. The Mohammedan priest who proposed the sacrifice had previously intimated to the chief that there was no danger of war coming to the town, but a few weeks after announced that "the books" had revealed that war was possible, but might be prevented by an offering of rice, cassava, fowls, etc., each village under the chief's influence contributing. When the people assembled at the appointed place and the articles brought were placed in a heap, the priest having charge of the ceremonies uttered a few sentences, the chief and people with hands stretched over the heap uttered the responses. During the ceremony I inquired of a friend who stood near me, "What will they do with these offerings?" "You will soon see, sir," was the reply. Then he explained that it is customary for the people at a given signal to rush upon the offering. "You will see plenty of fun for big and little people all tumble together, as everybody must try to get something of this sacrifice." I did not see this kind of fun, for the priest announced that the books further revealed that only Mahommedans should eat this offering. This was a surprise and a disappointment to the people, but not to the Mohammedans who had previous knowledge of this revelation, (?) for one immediately whispered to my friend, " I am glad for this, for we must soon starve if we no been do this thing."

§ XIII. SOCIETIES.

Organized societies are found among the tribes throughout the West coast. Among the Sherbros the Purroh is the most formidable institution. Its laws are binding upon chieftains and people alike. Until within recent years, the appearance of the Purroh messenger upon a scene of war between Sherbros, was to cause immediate cessation of hostilities, and an amicable settlement of difficulties. This *Purroh* must not be confounded with the various Purrohs (or unions) now found in sections of the country, for these are organized to gain specific ends. Boys and men are eligible to membership, and are sometimes forced into it. Their meeting place is in the grove, and none but members or those seeking membership can enter. Women, on pain of death, are forbidden to so much as look upon or pry into their workings. There are cases when one woman in a large district is admitted; when this is done, it is for a special purpose.

The *Boondoo* is a society for girls and women, but not as formidable as the Purroh, nor are its penalties as severe. The *Yassay* holds an important place. The *Thomah* is open to males and females. There are other local organizations. The most of these societies, like the Purroh, meet in groves, where none but members are permitted to enter. It is not my purpose to enlarge upon these societies, or to enter into their internal workings, for I have never entered a grove during their session, hence can not vouch for all I may have heard. It must be understood, however, that as missionaries, we oppose every institution of a heathen origin, whose workings are under cover of darkness. This fact is known to those among whom we labor. I am sure, too, that they in a measure respect our views.

A member of the Purroh and other societies was sick in one of our towns, and was expected to die. He had refused every invitation to attend religious services, hence at his death he could only look to his societies for his last comfort.

One day, while I was seated in a veranda of our mission house, I was startled by the sudden appearance of a man dressed in a garment covered with human bones, with a cap of human skulls on his head. He had learned of the serious illness of his brother, and had come to administer the last rites, to make sure of his burial, so that his bones might afterward be exhumed to be added to this horrible paraphernalia.

§ XIV. MISSIONARY EFFORTS.

It would be both profitable and interesting to trace the progress of the missionary idea as a work of God through the Church, Jewish and Christian, from its earliest establishment. But we must concede that the missionary spirit found a new life and impulse in the command of Christ, the great head of the Church: "Go ye therefore and teach all nations;" that is, make disciples, or Christians, of them. This command made in Galilee to a few chosen ones, resounded through every valley and along every hillside of Judea, till the inhabitants, awakened to the truth that "God is no respecter of persons," went forth to "teach the nations."

This command set free Jewish minds from the restraints of national prejudice, and forced them beyond their own domains, even across the sea, with the commission of their Lord. The nations heard the Gospel, and, arrested in their career, turned from their scenes of carnage and destruction to obey the mandate of heaven's king. If you in this land of blessed privileges and Gospel light, enjoy the blessing of life, liberty and happiness, it is because Christ's disciples, in obedience to these words of the Master, preached the Gospel to your ancestors. This command will not have lost its power or meaning to the Church till "the kingdoms of this world have become the kingdom of our Lord and His Christ."

The Church is bending its energies to this end. It remains for each individual to feel that he has a share in this work. It is my purpose in addressing you upon this subject to awaken, if possible, increased interest and confidence in foreign missionary work. I am aware that there are methods of viewing this subject that have led to unfair and uncharitable conclusions in regard to this work. Some, looking only at the amount annually expended, have failed to see adequate results of these expenditures, and have therefore concluded that the whole enterprise has not proved a success. Others again have said that the amount sent abroad might be turned to a better advantage in efforts to ameliorate the condition and help those whom they call "heathens at home,"—as if there is any necessity to have *heathens* in a land flowing with streams from the wells of salvation, where all who will may drink and live. Conclusions like these are not worthy a Christian, and are not such as I would draw from the teachings of Christ, who estimated the value of one soul to be worth more than the world's wealth. Nor does God, if His revelations in His word are true, limit this work to any particular place, people or time, or spare any efforts or means for the salvation of the human race. Even if it necessitated the gift of His only begotten Son, he resolved that "whosoever believeth in Him might not perish, but have everlasting life," it being nothing less than an eternal purpose that the Gospel of His kingdom be preached among all the nations before the end come. There can be but one method of viewing this subject, and no other is permissible; surely not to the Christian, who is bound to look upon it as God does, and view it in the same light.

But is it true that money sent or contributed to the foreign field has been vainly expended? Let me call attention to the following, from *The Missionary Review*:

"Comparing this percentage of increase of communicants in all the foreign missions (19.71) with the percentage of increase in Christendom

(.57), the difference is startling. It must be considered that our data for estimating this percentage in Christendom are far less complete than in case of the foreign mission; but with all proper allowance for this, the difference is still remarkable; and if we rightly understand its lessons, one of them is that instead of limiting Christian efforts to Gospel-hardened sinners in Christendom, Christ would have his last command obeyed— would have the knowledge and offer of salvation by his atoning blood speedily communicated to every individual of the race. This larger blessing from God on missions among the heathen, resulting in so much larger ingatherings of converts in heathendom than in Christendom, in proportion to the men and money employed in the two fields, is a fact which deserves the very serious and prayerful consideration of every believer, and especially of every young man entering the ministry."

The gain of one thousand converts in our mission during the past year, and of two thousand in the last three years bears testimony to the facts just quoted. These results have been attained at a great cost in money and sacrifice of lives. It cost something before the Saxons were won from their devotion to heathen deities and druidical sacrifices to become worshipers of the God of heaven, and by the influence of a Bible Christianity were made to become the dominant race of the world. There are *results* of missionary work that figures and statistics can not represent. The *influence* exerted upon a country by the mere presence of missionaries with the Bible; the vast number who, though not Christians or mentioned in reports, have been elevated by contact with missionaries; the number of children who are annually gathered in schools; the cultured men who hold positions of influence and power, and the effect of Christian literature upon communities where published, are matters which you can not gather from missionary reports. Then, too, you must not forget to estimate the *reflex influence* exerted upon the people of Christendom, together with the contributions made by missionaries to science, history, geography, and literature in general. Now, the poorest field in heathen countries sheds an influence that you and I dare not and can not estimate on this side of eternity. Dr. Thompson says he never knew how much to appreciate missionary work till he saw that work as done in places visited by himself and Dr. Hott during their travels in the East. He mentioned especially the mission at Beyroot, Syria, where was a splendid university sending out cultured men annually, some of whom not being Christians may never be mentioned in reports, who are yet holding places of trust and honor. All this is in addition to the Christian literature published in Arabic and in several dialects. I am glad, however, that the views of men are changing regarding the condition and need of the heathen world and the relation of the Church to the heathen, and that the old saying "Charity begins at home" has lost its force. Men realize that duty may begin at home, but charity, heaven's noblest and loveliest grace, expends herself abroad.

Africa has been for nearly a century the scene of earnest, faithful missionary work. There are many who have fallen as heroes in the conflict, and many have returned broken down in health. A wonderful providence has so guarded and preserved the lives of the missionaries of the Church of the United Brethren in Christ that during the thirty years of its operation in that land none have died in the field. All have had more or less severe afflictions, one returned to die among friends.

Among the Boards or societies, besides the United Brethren in Christ, actively represented on the West Coast are the Church Missionary Society, Society for Propagation of the Gospel in Foreign Parts, Wesleyan Methodists, Lutherans, Baptists, Congregationalists, Episcopalians, and Presbyterians. The work of Bishop Taylor, of the Methodist Church, should be watched with great interest. It is certainly a stupendous undertaking. The life and force that it must set in motion in the interior with what has been and is being accomplished on the coast, will enable us to look forward to the near fulfillment of Scripture when Ethiopia shall have stretched forth her hands unto God. The United Brethren in Christ are operating in five districts of the Sherbro country, Shaingay and Cockborough, Bompeh, Sherbro Island, Bargroo, and Impereh. These are advantageous positions, not only bringing besides Sherbros, representatives of other tribes under our immediate influence, but affording openings for a steadier advance into the interior. It is worthy of notice that persons from the interior tribes have already come in contact with our missionaries, and have heard from them the message of life. The wave being set in motion must extend and widen farther each year.

Many obstacles present themselves to the Church on the coast. These must be overcome before this glorious future is realized. But the gospel is equal to the task. It is the power of God unto salvation. You have seen from the description given you the dark side of African life, yet if Paul's description of the people of his day be true (Rom. I.), we have in Africa the same condition. To doubt the power of the gospel to meet this condition is to question God's great love and truthfulness. Then again if the past has any lesson in it as regards God's dealings with men and the changes that his word has wrought among the nations of the earth, we must believe that the same "Lord over all is rich unto all that call upon him." "But how shall they call on him in whom they have not believed, and how they believe in him of whom they have not heard, and how shall they hear without a preacher?" Religion is not *indigenous* to any particular country, nor is it especially adapted to any one climate. Wherever found it is *exotic*. Yet men talk and express doubts of the Christianization of Africa and Africans, as if certain nations have obtained from heaven a patent right to this gospel of Christ.

Another obstacle, and one demanding the serious consideration of those interested in the spread of Christianity, is the effect of the rum traffic among the people of the West Coast. Native wars would be less frequent, social life improved, and many miseries mitigated, but for the terrible effect of this cursed traffic. * Added to this is the unprincipled lives of some men from foreign countries who in those dark lands throw off the restraints of civilized life; and yet such are the men who are often loudest and most positive in their assertions that missionary work in heathen lands "does not amount to much," and who will point their finger in ridicule to the wrecks they have made and the powers they have blighted, and tell us "That is an example of your missionary converts. You can not make Christians of them," etc.

The results of missionary efforts and successes of the past ought to inspire confidence in every heart. Less than a century ago, missionary labor was commenced in Sierra Leone, on the West coast. When we take into consideration the condition of the people and the circumstances under which these labors were commenced, the results appear almost marvelous.

---

* The firm of Messrs. Yates & Porterfield, of New York, who are carrying on an extensive trade in Africa, not only do not engage in this traffic, but do not allow rum or liquors to be shipped to Africa in their vessels.. This is a worthy example, befitting Christian gentlemen.

Since writing the above, I have seen the following in a recent periodical: "We are glad to see that several of our prominent missionary societies, German, British, and American, are earnestly petitioning their respective governments to adopt measures for effectually restricting the importation and sale of liquors in Africa. We earnestly hope their petitions may prevail. The wretchedness and woe caused in Africa by the importation of distilled liquors are enough to bring the condemnation and curse of God on all who have engaged in this debasing crime, and on the nation and governments which have tolerated it."

When I left Africa fifteen years ago (1871), Freetown was the educational center. There were but few institutions that professed to teach more than the ordinary branches. On my return eight years after, great and rapid growth and improvement was manifest. I found several institutions under efficient native teachers, and the higher branches in English and the classics taught. Many of Africa's sons and daughters were seen crowding into these temples of learning.

The progress of religion has kept pace with the march of education, for as the young men became educated, the pulpits received better supplies. Ministers before who were barely able to read the Scriptures, have been replaced or improved by a talented ministry, men capable of interpreting the word. Men like Bishop Crowther, Quaker, Moore, Williams, May, Archdeacon Johnson, Pierce, Mark, and many others on the coast, can grace with dignity the pulpits of any country in Christendom.

Bishop Cheetham, in an address a few years since, mentioned in high terms the efficiency of the native ministry in Sierra Leone, and that "African pastors are so well sustained by their people, that there is no clerical poverty or destitution in Sierra Leone, as is to be feared prevails to a considerable extent in England." "Any one visiting Sierra Leone," he adds, "would find a land as thoroughly Christian as our own, whether that would be saying much or little. He would find a land of schools and chapels—a land of liberty and freedom." Freetown has to-day its barristers-at-law, its educated physicians, besides men in the various departments of the colonial government.

What is true of Sierra Leone is largely true of other portions of Africa. The various trades that have been acquired, the buildings constructed, all show the susceptibility of Africans of a high state of culture and development, morally, intellectually, physically. Sherbro, and particularly those portions that have been under our influence, have shown a remarkable change. Fifteen years ago, the question of giving up the Sherbro mission was strenuously discussed, for there was but one station, and that was faintly struggling for existence. Instead now of a single weak station, there are about three hundred towns and villages visited by our mission-aries, while nearly three thousand souls, once heathens, are believers in the one true God, and His Son, Jesus Christ. Schools have been opened, many have embraced the advantages afforded, and have shown themselves worthy of a higher and better education. With the limited education given them, some have been able to engage in business and trades, while a few are employed as teachers.

§ XV. PLANS AND METHODS.

Our plans and methods of work have given us an advantage that is even acknowledged by leading men of sister denominations in Sierra Leone, for our farm, mechanical and commercial industries, as well as the sound training given our youths, are fully adapted to the wants of the country. Besides, we have not been content with the work done in towns where our stations are located, but our plan is to visit each town and village within a certain area about each station, and there preach the word. In this way large districts have come under our influence.

§ XVI. A UNITED STATES OFFICER'S TESTIMONY.

Hon. Judson A. Lewis, United States Consul, resident at Sierra Leone, West Africa, a gentleman of vast experience and knowledge of the people on the coast, speaks in glowing terms of our work. After mentioning the efficient services rendered the Church and missions by Bishop D. K. Flickinger by his thorough knowledge of the needs of the field, owing to the Bishop's frequent visits to Africa, he adds: "Shaingay mission, which has been under the charge for eleven years of Rev. Joseph Gomer and wife, is a good and prosperous mission. Why? Because it is managed on business as well as religious principles. It is an industrial mission, where the boys and girls and all connected with it are regularly taught to do all kinds of work. The mission has a farm, and the boys do a certain number of hours' work on the farm every day, while the girls are as regularly taught to sew, to do house-work, patch-work, etc. The same boys and girls also attend the school, where they are taught the common English branches, and on Sunday their Sunday-school lessons.

"Now, the working part of the mission is all-important, and renders it largely self-supporting. Too much importance can not be attached to the labor department, for this renders them fit to do something in their own country and among their own people; what they learn under these circumstances they can not and will not forget, and should the mission be broken up and removed to-morrow, all the useful lessons that these boys and girls have learned by hard work, they will not readily forget."

3

XVII. COLONIZATION.

The work of a missionary, especially in a country like Africa, is both to civilize and to Christianize the people. We have seen that our success is based largely upon our combined religious, business, and industrial enterprises. But only a comparatively few can be brought under the direct influence of our schools. By far the greater number are beyond this influence and must be reached in some other way. I can conceive of no plan that would prove so effective as that of planting Christian colonies in various portions of the country, so that the masses as well as those under our instruction may be benefited by this contact with men and women from civilized or Christian countries. More can be learned from this object lesson, as to the order of a Christian home or family life and various methods of doing business, than from any instructions given by simply telling how this and that thing is done in civilized countries. The advantage to the country and people arising from this plan is next to having young men taken to this country or to Europe.

I object to colonization based upon the Liberian plan, as by it promiscuous classes were forced upon Africa, some being indigent and worthless, and not only a disgrace to America but a hindrance to true progress. What benefit could you hope to be derived from a people who were in many particulars inferior of the native African? Many have been the laughing stock of the natives. There are notable exceptions, it is true, but the present condition of Liberia shows what she has gained from this class of her citizens.

Send Christian men and their families, men of worth and principle, men of different trades and callings,—help them to settle in favorable localities and they would soon effect a change.

The exceeding unhealthfulness of the climate is often urged. While this is true, let me here state that the death rate among foreigners has decreased since men have learned that they can not live debauched and reckless lives with impunity ; and then, too, let us remember that America was not opened and settled without a terrible mortality among the first settlers.

To live in Africa you must have good homes in the most favorable localities, and great care as to mode of living and food must be maintained. Merchants and others are willing to risk Africa for money,—has not Christ any among his own who are willing to risk it in his name to gain precious souls ?

§ XVIII. MORE WORK FOR CHRIST.

These successes of the past are incentives to make the future grander in results and victories, and we should make use of and profit even by our failures and mistakes, so as to put into operation the best plans and make use of the most effective agencies to accomplish this end.

The heathen world is open to us. God in a most remarkable manner has opened the "world" to the preaching of the gospel. This he has done in China, Japan, Africa, and other places hitherto closed to a Christian missionary. This is doubtless due to the prayers of the Church as also to a fulfillment of God's promises, "I will give thee the heathen for thine inheritance," etc. Have we faith to follow in the path pointed to us? God has fulfilled many of his promises; will the Church, true to its God, consecrate its talent, its influence, and wealth? Could the tenth part of the wealth of the Church be consecrated to his cause it would not be long before the heathen world would have heard the gospel. I may be pardoned if I quote from a recent sermon delivered by Rev. Z. Warner, D. D., the missionary secretary:

"The papers say we spend $125,000,000 for dress each year. If this be true, then $25,000,000 are spent by Christians. We spend $25,000,000 for kid gloves. Of this amount $5,000,000 are spent by American·church people; $5,000,000 are spent for ostrich feathers, or $1,000,000 by Christians; $80,000,000 for tobacco, and of this amount more than $15,000,000 are spent by those who pray for the conversion of the world; $180,000,000 are spent in travel abroad by 60,000 Americans, and Christians spend their share. Add to this $900,000,000 for strong drink, and church people spend some of this, and you can see where much of this money goes. There is given to education $95,000,000, to Christian missions $5,000,000, and to the support of the church at home, $50,000,000.

If the annual income of the American church is $10,000,000,000, then there should be given to God $100,000,000 annually: This would give to the home work $75,000,000, and to foreign missions $25,000,000."

The souls to be won for Christ are many and precious. If heathens were not already conscious of their condition we might afford to move slowly, but the fact is the heathen not only is conscious of his need, not only feels that his objects of trust have failed him, but having learned of a God and a religion that saves, turns to the Church, and asks to be permitted to know something of that God.

Who will dare deny him the "Words of Life?" It is true that not all Africans have been awakened to this degree of consciousness, but as long as man has in him a soul, whose source is God, there must come a time when that soul must be conscious of its relation to God. This is true of individuals,—it is true of nations. This cry now heard upon Africa's shores is the echo of a universal wail, "Give us the time God or we must make a god for ourselves."

I call to mind an incident in missionary experience. An itinerant of our mission, while spending a night in one of the towns of his district, was awakened late in the night by the sound of foot-steps and noise about the door of his hut. His first thoughts were, "this must be a war party." But his fears were quieted when he heard a voice call "Soo-kool·massa! soo-kool-massa!" (school·master). Upon going out he found a goodly number of persons about the door, who were come to hear "God palaver." They had heard in their heathen village from two of their citizens, that a "God man" had talked "God palaver" in a town not far from them. These two men attempted to tell what they had heard, but their poor efforts only increased the desire to hear the word. This was the cause of their nocturnal visit. Who could resist this mute but eloquent appeal?

Ah, Christian friends, many such appeals have come to us that we could not heed. We have been pained to hear calls for the Gospel that we could not supply, for we have been compelled to limit our efforts to certain bounds. I do not know where God wants us to limit our work, and I have been alarmed when I have passed by places that needed the Gospel, for I somehow felt that God must call somebody to account for not giving it.

"We are not responsible for every heathen that dies, for all won't be saved, anyhow." You are not sure about that. If I was passing by a body of water, and should see some one drowning, and should throw in ropes or sticks or anything to help that drowning man, even if I did not succeed, and I saw him go from me and sink in the water, I say to you, though I may never forget the look of agony on that dying face, I should feel better because I had done something to save him. On the other hand, not all the melodies chanted by the heavenly choir could still the thunders of an accusing conscience, had I passed by without an effort to save him. Let me ask you, with the heathen world perishing in its sin against God, and the Master calling, can you, unawakened to their cries and deaf to His commands, yet feel that you have the enjoyment of Christ's love?

" Let none hear you idly saying,
There is nothing I can do,
While the souls of men are dying,
And the Master calls for you.
Take the task He gives you, gladly,—
Let His work your pleasure be;
Answer quickly when He calleth:
' Here am I; send me! send me!' "

In conclusion, let me urge you to take up as a battle-cry, "Sherbro for Christ!" God has led the Church into that territory, and we are there to stay. But to occupy that vast territory will require men and money. You supply the money, and God will raise the men. Fortunately for us, there are young men and women in Africa who are ready to enter the field if you give them the necessary preparation for the work. The training school to be opened shortly in Africa, has so much in its favor, and the advantages to be derived from it are so apparent, that I need not take the time to present them. But I want your boys and girls in the Sunday-school to set this school in motion. If we can get any fifty of you to give each five cents a month for three years, we could use that amount to educate a boy or girl in the school.

Many of you see the necessity for occupying the field, and yet you do not see how you can go, or give up your children to the work. This plan shows you how you can stay at home and yet serve the Master in heathen Africa. Let your contributions of books, clothing and money prove your interest in the salvation of the heathen and the extension of the Redeemer's kingdom.

www.ingramcontent.com/pod-product-compliance
Lightning Source LLC
Chambersburg PA
CBHW021604270326
41931CB00009B/1368